Stop Selling
and Start Closing

Stop Selling and Start Closing

*How to Close a
Real Estate Transaction
A Guide for New York
Real Estate Professionals*

Montana G. Spillman

To order additional copies of this book, contact:
Xlibris Corporation
1-888-795-4274
www.Xlibris.com
Orders@Xlibris.com
62745

Contents

Chapter Four

Real Estate Professional's Tools of the Trade

Chapter Five

How and Where Real Estate Professionals Find Listings

How and Where Real Estate Professionals Find Buyers

Chapter Six

Maintaining Your Edge in the Real Estate Market

Stop Selling and Start Closing is dedicated to my protégé, Diana Deluise, who has spent the last three years learning the real estate brokerage business under my tutelage and all my students who have requested that I publish a book depicting my experiences as a real estate professional.

Introduction

This book was written to be used as a training manual for the agents of Affluent Properties Group Corporation, a New York real estate brokerage corporation, and as a *self-help/how-to textbook* on closing real estate transactions in the real estate industry. The closing procedures and techniques I speak of in this book are drawn from my own forty plus (+) years of real estate experience. They are techniques and procedures that I have shared with my staff and are currently being used in training and application on a daily basis.

In the past twenty (20) years of my career as a real estate educator and instructor, I have become a mentor to many of my students and fellow licensees. Many of whom have expressed to me not only a deep desire but also a personal need to be trained and cross-trained in closing techniques in real estate sales. All of whom have at some point in our relationship inquired about a specific class that I may be aware of, or a *self-help/how-to book* they could read that would help them develop the necessary skill to successfully sell and close real estate transactions consistently.

Because I have been repeatedly asked to recommend classes and books that would build their confidence and create the self-esteem necessary to achieve financial success in selling real estate, I have set aside the time to share my experiences as a real estate professional on the subject of successfully closing real estate transactions.

Although the legal issues involved in drawing the contract of sale and the delivery of a valid deed are in most instances similar or the same, this book concentrates on the techniques and procedures it takes to arrive at that place in time where the buyers and the sellers sign the contract of sale.

It is through the diligent efforts of real estate professionals that a sales transaction is put into motion. It is the real estate professional and a competent closing team that supply the inertia that keeps the transaction in motion until it closes.

It is imperative that new real estate agents learn this procedure so that they create a cash flow and become financially successful in the real estate industry.

Most real estate offices train their new agents, thus supplying the education and experience necessary to enjoy a successful career. The key to a successful career, as is in any profession, is education. This success is often predicated on the real estate school chosen by them for an alma mater. As in the choice of a school for any profession, there are real estate schools. When a real estate school is chosen based solely on the cost of tuition, one must consider the old adage, "You get what you pay for." The real estate school of choice supplies another key to success, as it is often the origin of a network that will eventually assist you in building your new career.

While I still have your attention, consider another old adage if you will: "Surround yourself with like-minded people and you will get like-minded results."

Of course I am aware that you may realize this can work against you as well; so let me add, in choosing the people you carefully surround yourself with, do not consider so much what they say but rather put more credence on how they communicate what is said and their overall performance of the day-to-day business activities.

First and foremost, this book addresses the need to close real estate transactions consistently by using specific methods, techniques, and proven procedures that will leave all the parties involved satisfied and well served.

The information in this book, if properly adapted and applied, will also leave you as a real estate professional, confident in your skill and ability to close a real estate transaction. This book will teach you how to set realistic and attainable goals, which will supply the motivation needed to give you regular, consistent, and positive results.

This book also teaches you the best way to generate more listings and attract new buyers, which will result in building your business, operating at your utmost capacity and functioning at your full potential by simply using the available tools of the trade consistently every day.

This book points out how you, the agent, can control the closing of a real estate transaction in whatever capacity you set out to represent a seller or a buyer. The relationship that you developed at first substantive contact is the key to the closing, whether you are a listing agent, a buyer agent, or a subagent in any capacity. This book illuminates the fact that there must be a relationship of trust formed between the agent and whoever the agent has brought into the real estate transaction. This book will teach you how to acquire wealth through real estate and how to maintain your health to enjoy the fruits of your labor. It will serve as an instructional manual and help to guide you throughout your career—from a new licensee to a real estate professional.

About the Author

New York State licensed real estate broker, HUD broker, real estate investor, real estate developer, educator, professor, author and motivational speaker, one of the original founders of Affluent Properties Group Corporation and is currently serving as the CEO.

Montana G. Spillman

Professional Affiliations

The author's professional affiliations are: National Association of Realtors, New York State Association of Realtors, Westchester County Board of Realtors, Westchester Putnam Multiple Listing Service, the Greater Hudson Valley Multiple Listing Service, National Notary Association, National Artist and Writers Guild, National Christian Writers and Poet's Fellowship, and National Association for the Advancement of Colored People.

Professional Awards

Since 1979, he was a subject of biographical record in the Barons Who's Who in American Real Estate in which inclusion is limited to those individuals who have demonstrated outstanding achievement, superior leadership, and exceptional service in the American real estate profession.

He was nominated an honorary trustee to the American Indian Relief Council in 1996.

Since June of 2002, he was placed on the Wall of Tolerance, honoring those who are leading the way toward a more tolerant and just America as founding members of the National Campaign for Tolerance.

Chapter One

Closing the Sale as a Buyer Agent

I.   The Relationship of the Buyer Agent's Interview with
      the Buyer and Closing the Transaction

The interview with the buyer begins with signing the first (1st) substantive contact agency disclosure form. In New York State, all residential real estate transactions for the sale or rental of a one (1) to four (4) family/unit residence must start with this New York State mandatory disclosure form.

Second, the agent must get the buyer to obtain a mortgage preapproval, which I recommend over a prequalification, from a lending institution of their choice or a mortgage broker that is a part of the agent's closing team.

The third step actually begins the closing process; this is where the agent finds out what the buyer has in mind in terms of the total investment, the location of the property, the type of property, a list of the properties they have already viewed, the reason and necessity for the purchase, and the time frame the buyer is committed to making the purchase. This also prevents a waste of valuable time and a clash with other agents the buyers has worked with in the past or is still currently working.

Whereas all of this information is essential, getting the buyer to commit to the necessity, as well as the time frame of the purchase, is vital to the agent in closing the sale when a property is located that meets as many of the buyer's requirements. It is at this time that the agent could, if it became necessary, without seeming too pushy, reiterate the buyer's requirements of the property to qualify for purchase if the buyer procrastinated when it came time to make the offer.

II. The Importance of the Buyer's Agent Informing the Buyer of What to Expect During the Sales Transaction and the Time Frame of the Process Between the Accepted Offer and the Closing

It is of equal importance for the agent to inform the buyer of how the process will work from offer to closing. It is at this time that the buyer should be informed of all of the real estate professionals who will be needed to close the sale, including the name of the attorney whom the buyer intends to use at closing. Some buyers will not be willing or simply not be able to provide this information at this point in the process. So it is imperative that the agent make the buyer understand the competition in the marketplace that they will face upon making an offer on a property that meets their needs and requirements. The buyer must be made to understand that having a closing team in place will provide them the best assurance of successfully closing the sale in a timely manner.

The fourth step in the process is the search for the right property that meets the buyer's requirements. This is best achieved by the agent's knowledge of the marketplace and a computer-generated search of the available appropriate properties.

Agents must understand that at this time in the process, the buyer is not committed to working with them exclusively. This being said, it is essential to build a working relationship between the buyer and the agent as soon as possible. This working relationship will be predicated on how quickly the agent begins to show and the buyer begins to view qualified properties currently for sale on the market.

III.   The Buyer Agent's Understanding of How and When to Obtain the Buyer's Offer

As you have read previously in the interview with the buyer, the buyer has been informed of how the process works from offer to closing. This gives the agent an edge when asking for the offer. The offer must be made as soon as the buyer shows an interest in the property. The agent should have been overtly reviewing the offering process with the buyer after viewing each property shown and discussing how each property fits the buyer's needs. If this process is adhered to, it should eliminate the unacceptable properties, leaving the possibly acceptable properties to be reviewed again if necessary.

Once the buyer gives the agent permission to make the offer to the seller, the agent must overcome another obstacle in the offering process—the listing agent. Yes, as strange as it may sound, the listing agent is often the reason why an offer is not accepted and sometimes never even made to the seller. Unfortunately, the only advice I can offer a new agent about overcoming this particular obstacle is experience; it comes over time and eventually you will get know which agents and agencies to avoid if you expect to consistently close your transactions.

IV.   The Buyer's Agent Negotiating the Buyer's Offer with the Listing Agent and the Principal, the Property's Seller

In New York, according to Article 12A of the Real Property Law, all offers are to be carried to the principal (seller) for acceptance or rejection. Whereas I indicated this was not always the case,

I am sure that it is done in most instances. The previous caveat was intended for new agents who have never encountered this particular problem.

Before showing a property, a buyer agent should call the selling agent for a conversation about the listing and a preview of the property. This procedure can sometimes prevent misunderstandings between agents and assists the agents in making a successful offer. The better we get to know each other as agents, the smoother our interoffice transactions tend to be progressed. This is something I believe to be true, and my staff and I do it as a matter of course.

All offers should be made in writing, faxed to the listing agent, and followed up with a telephone call to confirm that the offer was received. The two agents should communicate the pros and cons of the offer within twenty-four (24) hours. This communication is a simple courtesy callback even if the offer was not countered or accepted. It is also the opportunity to tell a fellow agent about any listings you may have or to extend an invitation to one of the agency's open houses.

If the listing agent does not return the buyer agent's telephone call within a twenty-four-hour (24) period, the buyer agent should call again, this time on the listing agent's cell phone. At this point in the offer, the buyer agent should inform the selling agent of the possibility of missing the opportunity of a sure sale from a qualified buyer.

This call usually gets a response from the listing agent, whether or not the response is positive or negative; it allows the buyer agent to move on and know that every possible thing was done to explore the sale in the best interest of the buyer. Remember, processing and eliminating all options and opportunities is an enormous part of the real estate business. The buyer agent must move quickly to turn a negative situation into a positive situation. Keep the buyer viewing new properties and reviewing properties that were of lesser interest but may have been a second or third choice. This is why the buyer agent must never give a negative opinion about a property, unless they are purposely using the negative-sell ploy; it may end up being the property that the buyer settles for based upon timing, location, and availability.

The negative-sell ploy is effective only when the agent is sure that the buyer wants the property based on a lower price, an unsatisfactory inspection, or it is the only property on the market that can be adapted to meet the buyer's needs and requirements. These facts can make the property a good find and a great buy for that particular buyer.

Remember the old adage, "The best property is a sold property." This adage is always true when it is you who sold the property.

Chapter Two

Closing the Sale as a Listing Agent

I.   The Relationship of the Listing Presentation to the Property's Seller and the Ability of the Listing Agent to Close the Transaction (15)

The listing agent must prepare a comparative market analysis before making the listing presentation. This is a computer-generated report of the competition the subject property will face in the market. It is comprised of like-kind properties that have been listed for sale, expired, as well as ones that have been sold within a (3) three- to (6) six-month period. These listing are called comparables or comps. The listing agent should also have at least (3) three to (6) six listings that were sold recently in the agent's office to validate his presence in the industry.

This report is used to establish a listing price for the subject property. A completed listing agreement should accompany the CMA report, prepared for the seller's signature in advance. This will show the seller the listing agent's confidence in selling the property in the time frame indicated in the listing agreement.

The listing agent should provide the seller with a résumé consisting of all the properties that have been listed and sold in his office to date. This information can be very impressive and is often the only reason the seller signs the listing agreement. A listing agent should get an exclusive right to sell listing agreement for at least six (6) months. This will give the property listed enough exposure in the marketplace and increase the agent's chance of selling the property. At this point in the presentation, pictures of the property and measurements of the rooms must be taken to provide the maximum visual exposure on the Multiple Listing Service and other related Internet Web sites.

II.   The Relationship of the Listing Agent Who is Negotiating the Buyer's Offer with the Property's Seller and Closing the Transaction

It is imperative to the closing of the sale that the seller is confident of the listing agent's competence and knowledge of the market. The listing agent is the key to getting the seller to accept the buyer's offer of sale. This confident relationship, established at the listing presentation, builds and escalates over the time frame of the listing agreement through communications and conversations pertaining to the sale of the property. It is the listing agent's responsibility to get the best possible selling price for the seller, depending upon the condition of the market and the necessity of the seller to sell at the time the offer of sale is received. This means the listing agent is obligated to present each and every offer of sale to the seller. The listing agent must carefully determine the best price and the best terms of every offer presented to the seller during the time frame of the listing. Considering the fiduciary responsibility given to the listing agent by the seller in the listing agreement, everyone concerned in the sale of the property is relying on the listing agent's ethics and competence in the acceptance of an offer process.

III. The Relationship of the Listing Agent to the Property's Seller and His Ability to Obtain a Counteroffer and Close the Transaction

The listing agent is responsible to the seller for obtaining counteroffers from buyers whose offers are lower than the seller's expectations. No offer of sale should be considered insulting to sellers and if they are, listing agents are remiss in their duty as fiduciaries of the seller if they do not encourage dialogue by presenting all the best aspects of the property to the offeror or the offeror's agent, thus working a lower-than-acceptable offer into an accepted offer, resulting in closing the transaction of sale.

Chapter Three

Closing the Sale as a Real Estate Professional

I. The Education of a Real Estate Professional

The choice of alma maters may be the difference in success and failure based upon the network system that every successful real estate professional must have in place. Being a real estate educator, I encourage anyone who is interested in becoming a new real estate salesperson to register in any one of the schools where I teach. I do this for several reasons. First and foremost, since I teach the initial real estate salesperson's course, I can guarantee the student an excellent education.

The second reason is that my students have access to me by telephone or e-mail as a resource for information and advice for their entire real estate career.

The third reason may be more advantageous than the first two since every two years, the state of New York mandates continuing education. These mandated courses give us a better handle on what we have already learned and are currently practicing in the field. They offer the knowledge necessary to practice real estate so that we can continue perfecting our profession. Last of all, these courses assist us in building, maintaining, and strengthening our network, which is essential to the success of all real estate professionals.

II.   The Development of a Positive and Result-Oriented Mentality

When you choose a career in sales, it's not only essential to know the product you are selling, but you must also believe in the product you're selling. This is especially true in the sale of real estate, amplified by the possession of a positive, result-oriented mentality.

Positive attitudes and result-oriented mentalities are not acquired by passing a state real estate exam and being issued a real estate license. These are something that must be developed over a period in conjunction with work-related experience and work ethics. It's about seeing it, believing it, achieving it.

A real estate professional must first be able to recognize an opportunity when it arises, have faith in the skills they have acquired through experience, and work diligently to make the transaction happen. This is the mind-set that produces the success that results from staying focused until all contingencies have been met and the transaction closes. It is at this time in the life of real estate professionals that they come to realize luck is for losers.

III.   Developing a Business Plan

The old adage "If you fail to plan, you plan to fail" rings true in any business venture. This effect is the biggest factor in the failure rate of real estate agents. The difference between real estate agents and real estate professionals is that real estate professionals treat their listing and customers as if they were in business for themselves. In the case of ordinary real estate agents, few if any, develop a business plan; on the other hand, real estate professionals understand that because they are operating their own business, a business plan is essential to their success.

A business plan is simply an outline of expectations for your business over a period of time. The business plan of a real estate professional working under the license of a principal broker should be developed around the principal broker's business plan.

The real estate professional's business plan does not have to be as detailed or as long ranged as the principal broker's business plan but must definitely be as committed.

The outline of the business plan must consist of goals and commitments in a specific time frame that the real estate professional has developed to achieve their expectations.

The best way to begin is with an income goal. Only you can determine how much you will need to sustain yourself and your family. Once you have determined the set amount of income necessary, the next question must be answered, "How do I achieve my income goal selling real estate?"

Real estate income is earned and paid out in commissions after a sale, lease, or rental (which is referred to as a transaction) is closed. This may take anywhere from forty-five (45) days to six (6) months, depending on the type of real estate transaction.

It could take new licensees a year or more to get their businesses to produce sufficient cash flows to achieve their income goal.

The income goal depends entirely upon the number and quality of the agent's property listings and buyers. The listings are the inventory that fuels the real estate brokerage industry, and the buyers ignite the desire to use property as a vehicle to gain personal wealth. These two factors keep the fires burning, creating the two cycles in which the real estate brokerage industry is totally dependent on—a seller's market or a buyer's market. Therefore, real estate professionals do not use the negative term *bad market*. We are in either a *seller's market* or a *buyer's market*.

The listings and buyer's goal must not only project the number of listings and buyers expected to fuel the business but also how and where to find them.

The next goal is to develop a real estate work schedule operating around your primary source of income. Making the time to become successful is the most important and sometimes the most difficult of all of the goals to achieve.

It is for this reason that for most real estate professionals, it all began as a dream—a dream so real it could be seen, a dream so real it could be believed, a dream so real it could be achieved. If you can understand what I'm saying, then this book is worth far more than the price you paid for it.

Which brings to mind the question that was asked of me in my first real estate brokerage interview, "Are you seeking full-time or part-time employment?"

I responded with the eloquent arrogance of who I believed myself to be, "I'm not looking for a job, I'm in search of my future. I'm starting my own real estate business, and I need your broker's license to manage my overhead. I'm here to discuss an independent contract agreement with percentages in both our best interest."

Needless to say, this approach was not immediately embraced, and I was politely shown the door upon more than one occasion. I don't recommend this approach to anyone seriously seeking an interview for immediate employment. However, it did eventually work for me because I brought with me a network of buyers and sellers who were, at that time, largely ignored in the real estate market.

I said this to make the most important point you will ever need to know about being hired to sell real estate: Bring a network of potential buyers and sellers along with you, and most probably you will be hired.

In seeking employment in the real estate profession, one must answer a very important question; the answer to which may get you the employment you are seeking.

Most potential employers will ask if you are thinking of doing real estate full-time or part-time. This is a question in which you must put much thought to make the right decision for yourself. You must ask yourself, "Can I do real estate full-time and earn enough income to support myself?"

Most people cannot practice real estate without having another job or source of income. The answer to this question is also the answer to why there is such a high rate of turnover and burnout in the real estate profession. Although I am addressing the problem here among the people it will affect first and foremost, this is a huge problem for real estate broker-managers. My thoughts are that the problem is self-inflicted by insisting that as a condition of employment a new agent must commit to full-time.

Practicing real estate is not a full-time job; practicing real estate is an obsession. True real estate professionals live, breathe, eat, and drink real estate twenty-four (24) hours a day, seven (7) days a week. Practicing real estate feeds the fire that sates the desire that drives them to own, buy, and sell real property. The people of which I speak are driven by an infinite, burning passion to succeed, spending all of their time seeking out real estate opportunities. Real estate professionals locate the financing, find the buyers, create partnerships, and close real estate transactions. Real estate professionals are not seeking employment; they seek out and create real estate opportunities. The true real estate professional invests and buys multi-unit properties that create income and cash flow. Whatever properties real estate professionals cannot raise the financing to buy, they sell to other buyers and collect a commission from the seller. These commissions are the seed money used to create down payments and/or closing cost to buy more properties for their financial portfolio. This modus operandi is what separates the few true real estate professionals in our industry from the majority of real estate licensees in the marketplace.

IV. Developing a Closing Team

Your closing team should consist of several attorneys, mortgage brokers, title companies, home inspectors, and exterminators licensed to kill wood-eating insects. This will give you the ability to offer the buyer a choice of real estate professionals to guarantee a successful closing. The most important member of the closing team is the mortgage broker. The mortgage broker qualifies the buyer for financing. The mortgage broker is the key factor in locating a lending institution that will offer the best programs, lowest interest rates, and terms—such as percentage of down payment, credit scores that are in the best interest of the buyer—and produce an unconditional commitment within a reasonable time frame in which to close the transaction.

Next is the buyer's choice of attorneys. The buyer should hire an attorney who is experienced in closing real estate transactions expeditiously, competently, and with whom they have negotiated a predetermined closing fee. I make it a rule not to suggest the monetary value of another real estate professional's services. I believe the value of the service rendered speaks for itself; the proof is how every obstacle in the transaction was overcome, which resulted in a successful closing.

The buyer's attorney will receive a contract of sale prepared by the seller's attorney, review it with the buyer before signing, and return it with the agreed-upon down payment stated in the contract. Soon thereafter, the buyer's attorney will order the title search and the survey of the property. The mortgage broker will have already delivered the mortgage commitment, or it will follow in a timely manner, at which time a closing date will be set by the seller, buyer, and bank attorneys.

Although the home inspector is the last real estate professional I mention on the closing team, he is usually the first one the buyer will hire after the real estate agent has located a suitable property to buy. The home inspector is usually misunderstood by real estate licensees and is widely referred to as the deal breaker by many.

However, we, whom I have referred to as the few among us, find his services to be essential and hold him in the highest regard. Few, if any, properties—newly constructed or built many years ago—are flawless. It is the job of the home inspector to point out these flaws and conditions. He prioritizes the severity, sets a timetable for the corrections, and indicates a probable cost that the buyer could incur if the property is purchased in its present condition.

This is done through a written home inspection report, presented to the buyer along with a bill for his services. The buyer will need the written home inspection report for his attorneys' review and possibly to be used to renegotiate the offer of sale by adjusting the selling price to the cost of correcting the flaws and conditions in the home inspection report.

The real estate professional thoroughly understands that this report is simply another tool used to establish the final selling price in the transaction. Because the listing agent has prepared the seller for this probability in the listing presentation, it comes as no surprise and is just another point to be negotiated for the sale to close.

Chapter Four

Real Estate Professional's Tools of the Trade

I.   The Tools Necessary for a Real Estate Professional to be Productive

Reliable automobile, home office, personal computer, laptop, flash/zip drive, digital camera, membership to Boards of Realtors and Multiple Listing Services, measuring instrument, business cards, and real estate signs.

II.   Using Real Estate Signs as Selling and Listing Tools

All agents should own their own real estate signs. All agents should promote their listings with real estate For Sale signs. A real estate For Sale sign should always include the agent's picture. This will not only promote the listed property, but also the listing agent and the real estate agency as well. The real estate For Sale sign should also be supported with smaller signs that attach to the larger sign, such as Sold, In Contract, Open House, Shown by Appointment or anything else you want to bring to the attention of the consuming public.

Billboards, bus shelters, trains, subways, and bus signs are also used for promoting real agencies and their agents. These signs can be effectively used in supermarkets, transportation centers, and theaters or any place where there is a captive audience. Remember the old Chinese proverb, "One picture is worth a thousand words."

Remember, advertising and promotion is the responsibility of the listing real estate agent and is only limited by experience and imagination.

Chapter Five

How and Where Real Estate Professionals Find Listings

I.   For Sale by Owner (FISBOs)

FISBO is an acronym meaning "for sale by owner." The FISBO is one of the best methods a real estate professional can use to secure a listing. This is evidenced by the following facts:

a. The owner of the property is already committed to selling the property by putting an advertisement in the printed media and/or a For Sale sign on the property for the public to see.

b. The owner of the property has invested money into marketing the property. In most instances, the owner has invested this money without getting a successful return on the dollars invested, which simply means the owner was unable to secure a qualified buyer and the money spent was wasted.

c. The owner of the property may or may not have had offers of sale for the property. However, there is one fact the real estate professional is sure of—the property has not been sold. There may have been several reasons that prevented the property from being sold thus far.

1. The owner of the property may not know how to market the property properly.
2. The owner of the property may not be able to qualify potential buyers.
3. The owner of the property may have had a bad experience with a real estate broker.

d. The owner of the property listed the property with a real estate broker who marketed property unsuccessfully.

Whereas none of these scenarios sound like positive selling points to secure a listing, a true real estate professional understands the most important point in the previous list of scenarios. The fact remains that in most instances, property owners will lose money when they try to market property without the assistance of a real estate professional. When real estate agents come to this realization, they tend to increase their listing productivity, methodically achieving their goals, creating the consistency needed to successfully become a real estate professional.

II. Expired Listings

Expired listings are properties that were listed by their owners with real estate agencies but have not been sold for several possible reasons: (a) the listed price was above market value, (b) the properties' owners unreasonably refused to lower the listing price to its true market value, or (c) the listing agent was unable to successfully market the property in the time frame in the listing agreement.

All of the previous reasons for an expired listing are really listing agent's excuses for losing the listing. None of these events should have occurred if the listing agent had paid careful attention to page 15, chapter 2, subtopic I, titled "The Relationship of the Listing Presentation to the Property's Seller and the Ability of the Listing Agent to Close the Transaction."

III. Search for Specific Properties to List Requested by the Buyers

An agent listening to a buyer's request for location and the type of property that the buyer desires is as important to a real estate professional as qualifying the buyer for a mortgage. This is most often accomplished by a computerized search using the Multiple Listing Service. However, the search for a specific property in a specific area is another method used for locating the right property for your buyer to purchase.

This can be accomplished by one of three methods: (a) a bulk mailing in which the listing agent hopes to find several properties to list, (b) a telephone marketing campaign, and (c) a door-to-door solicitation campaign.

The bulk mailing campaign is a listing method that should be done once a year whether there is a specific buyer in mind or not. This will produce two means to an end: (a) name recognition, and (b) a property listing.

The telephone solicitation method is a tedious endeavor in which the agent wants to make contact with a possible seller and must be careful not to become an annoyance, not to mention, chance a violation of Department of State Nonsolicitation Order 178.5 prohibited forms of solicitation, which could achieve the opposite effect of the name recognition campaign.

Personally, I find the door-to-door solicitation campaign far more effective. When contact is made, you have the advantage of speaking to someone face-to-face and developing an instant relationship, whether it is positive or negative. On the other hand, if contact is not made, you can leave some kind of literature behind advertising yourself, your agency, and your services. Again I must remind you of violating the DOS Nonsolicitation laws.

How and Where Real Estate Professionals Find Buyers

I.   Referrals from Satisfied Buyers and Sellers

Every buyer must receive a housewarming gift upon closing the transaction. There is no better method for developing new business than a referral from a satisfied buyer or seller. This can be encouraged by mailing out special event cards after the closing, such as birthday, Christmas, Thanksgiving, Easter, etc. Make sure a business card with your picture is in every card sent. Remember the old Chinese proverb, "One picture is worth a thousand words."

II.   New Agents and Self-Promotion

However, new agents must promote themselves with announcements by mail and other printed media such as business cards with pictures. I recommend that new agents distribute at least a thousand (1,000) business cards per month to promote themselves in the first year of business. This means that family and friends must be committed to their success. Everyone the new agent knows should be given business cards to distribute to everyone they know. This is the total commitment your family and friends must make to you. All of this and more is necessary for your success in the real estate brokerage industry.

Chapter Six

Maintaining Your Edge in the Real Estate Market

I.   Business Begets Business and Using Other Agents to Build Your Business

Successful real estate professionals are so busy concentrating on the goals they have set for themselves that it is almost impossible to achieve these goals on their own.

A successful real estate professional must have an assistant—in fact as many assistants as possible; use other agents to help build your business. It is well-advised to mentor new agents, and use them as assistants until they develop their businesses.

Hundreds of new agents are being licensed every week. Not all real estate brokerages have the ability to train agents; they hire them and let them find their own way around the marketplace. These new agents are untrained, nonproductive, and end up not renewing their licenses due to a combination of lack of time and the DOS mandatory requirement of twenty-two-and-a-half hours of continuing education. It's imperative that real estate professionals keep abreast of the changing DOS requirements for licensure.

II.   Using Your Commissions to Create Wealth by Acquiring Property

If real estate professionals are going to make any real money in this industry, they must create streams of income. This can be accomplished by using the commissions earned to buy multi-unit properties. Commissions, depending upon the amount, can be used for down payments or to pay the closing cost in real estate transactions. Successful real estate professionals are not only real estate brokerage agents but are also landlords and property managers. By exploring other aspects of the real estate industry, they increase their income potential from finite to infinite.

III.   Understanding the Connection Between Health and Wealth

It has been said that "money isn't everything." Whereas this statement is definitely true, it's usually made by people who have money, which makes it easy for them to say this since they are not in dire need of it.

It is also said that "if you have your health, you have everything." This statement is also a definite truth. When it is made by a wealthy person who is sick, it's a tale of woe. When it is made by a person who is poor, it is usually a tale of regret that they are not wealthy.

It is imperative for successful real estate professionals to know that wealth is attained and health is maintained, so one is nothing without the other. In other words, they are perfect partners. We have already talked about creating streams of income, which will eventually lead to attaining this wealth; if I remember correctly, we referred to it as infinite wealth.

Let us now talk about maintaining health so we can enjoy infinite wealth. Health is maintained with a routine of proper daily exercise. This must be in conjunction with a healthy well-balanced diet—another set of the perfect partners essential to maintaining infinite health.

In summary, we must add another goal to our business plan, one that we must be just as committed as we are to the others: a health goal. In short, real estate professionals must form a partnership with wealth, health, exercise, and diet to be truly successful in their chosen career.

IV.   Tracking Your Progress

When one sets a goal, one must also create a chart to track the progress. This can be divided into two (2) parts: short-term goals and long-term goals. Both set of goals must be set in a time frame of expectations. Short-term goals can be daily, weekly, or monthly. Long-term goals are usually annual goals and are measured by the previous year's income. Real estate broker managers use this as a tool to motivate their sales force and track their annual sales. Incentives and recognition of milestones and accomplishments are also necessary for the growth of the business.

V.   Weekly Office Meeting and Agent Reports

Real estate professionals must attend weekly office meetings and submit a weekly and monthly progress report to their managers. The weekly meeting has a threefold purpose: (a) educational, (b) motivational, and (c) internal networking.

Education is first and foremost in the success of a real estate professional. A real estate professional must be able to communicate by developing their writing skills as well as their verbal skills. The real estate brokerage business has developed into the communication business; there is no place for computer illiterates in our business.

Motivation is the energy produced by the driven few to succeed by creating jobs, cash flow, and streams of income from multiple sources.

Internal networking is the sharing of resources and ideas that cause anyone who comes into contact with you to prosper just by having the opportunity to know you.

VI.   Keeping Records for Income Tax Purposes

Real estate professionals are independent contractors, which means that no taxes are deducted from the commissions paid out by the principal broker. Real estate professionals receive a 1099-MISC tax form and pay taxes on any commissions over six hundred ($600) dollars received from the employing brokerage firm. A real estate professional is expected to pay quarterly taxes to the IRS to avoid having an excessive tax burden at the end of the tax year. This can also be accomplished by keeping records and receipts of all taxable expenditures related to real estate sales in any given tax year.

All real estate professionals should have a certified public accountant to identify and qualify their taxable expenditures. Items that may be considered are car mileage, gas, repairs and maintenance, tolls, parking, and car washes. In some instances and circumstances, a percentage of your home office and supplies can be deductible.

The accountant may depreciate the home office equipment and furniture over the allowable period of time. A reasonable understanding of the IRS tax laws should be an essential part of every real estate professional's education. I would like to make it perfectly clear that all advice related to taxes should come from an accountant of your choice.

The Author's Closing Thoughts

I am sure the information you have received after having read my book will supply the motivation for developing the necessary skills to become confident, consistent closers in the real estate industry.

However, if you have paid close attention to what I said, you would have realized by now that my formula for success is deeply rooted in personal property investment. My book's message is to invest capital earned through real estate commissions into relatively low-risk real estate ventures for the sole purpose of developing income-producing properties and creating cash flow, coupled with the thorough knowledge of how to make long-term real estate investments produce positive returns for your future.

My formula for success is based on foresight, which at best, is a limited glimpse into the shadows of an unforeseen future with a narrow, restricted view. This is a future in which the elders among us have personally experienced and the youth among us have put their faith into—a future in which those who fear to invest become the self-appointed prophets of doom, pinpointing the pitfalls and predicting devastating failure for the real estate professionals who dare to take the chance.

The truth is, it's a gamble based on calculated risks, risks which are limited by the extent of the professional real estate investor's education and vision of the future. The prophets of doom have tried to diminish the victory of the faithful few by proclaiming foresight to be hindsight 20/20 vision. But only after those who dared to put my formula to the test, tilled the soil and sowed the seeds of their faith in a real estate cycle entrenched in a hostile financial environment, and successfully endured the responsibilities of property stewardship will harvest the fruits of their labor.